The author's thanks to Frank H. Forrester, of the American Museum-Hayden Planetarium, New York, for his suggestions regarding the manuscript of this book.

FIFTH PRINTING

Library of Congress Catalog Card Number: 56-5851

Printed in the United States of America by Polygraphic Company of America, Inc.

Published in Canada by Ambassador Books, Ltd., Toronto 1, Canada

THE **FIRST BOOK** OF

WEATHER

by **ROSE WYLER**

pictures by **BERNICE MYERS**

FRANKLIN WATTS
NEW YORK

contents

1. the air around you

"Rain tomorrow," says the weatherman. When you hear the forecast, the sky is clear and blue. But when morning comes, rain is pouring from thick gray clouds.

How did the weatherman know the storm was coming? Did he just happen to make a good guess? Well, look at his score. It's better than you think. Eight or nine times out of ten, the forecasts are right. As one weatherman put it:

> These in the main are my regrets:
> When I am right, no one remembers;
> When I am wrong, no one forgets.

Weathermen do not depend on hunches. They are scientists. They know that air changes from hour to hour, from day to day, and that the changes cause weather. They know that storms build up gradually. Each day they watch for changes in the winds, clouds, temperature, dampness, and heaviness of the air. These clues tell them what tomorrow's weather will be.

1

You can learn to understand these changes, too, and make your own forecasts. This book tells how. All you need is a thermometer and a few things from your own kitchen. You can even start forecasting now. Just say, "Today's weather will not last," and you're sure to be right.

Knowing what air is made of will help you understand why weather is always changing. Air is a mixture of invisible gases. Clouds drift through the mixture; and particles of smoke, dust, pollen, and sea salt float among the gases. But they are not air. **Oxygen,** the gas you must breathe to keep alive, and another gas called **nitrogen** make up most of the mixture. Air also contains traces of several other gases and some **water vapor,** the invisible gas that forms when water "dries up." To a weatherman the most important of these gases is water vapor, for all clouds, rain, and snow form from it.

Each gas is made of its own special kind of tiny particles, called **molecules.** The different molecules are mixed, so that a batch of air in one place is very much like a batch of air anywhere else. All the molecules are unbelievably small. Two million of them placed in line would hardly stretch across a grain of table salt.

Air molecules are lively things. They dart up, down, and sideways, moving at different speeds. Sometimes they bump into one another, but usually there is plenty of space between them. If the molecules were to crowd close together, they would not form air, but a mixture of liquids and solids. Imagine trying to breathe that!

The gases of the air have no color, yet as sunlight passes through trillions of their molecules, the sky turns blue. This is why. Sunlight is a mixture of different rays, each a color of the rainbow. Together, the rays make white light. Although rays of all colors get through the air, a good many of the blue rays are stopped by the gas molecules and scattered around. Their scattering makes the blue of the sky.

Ten or more miles above the earth, a pilot must look down, not up, to see the sky's blueness. It appears as a filmy, colored veil covering the earth. Above the pilot the sky is a dark purple. Higher than 15 miles it is just as black in the daytime as at night. The reason for this is that sun rays light up the sky only after striking air molecules, and these thin out gradually.

About nine tenths of the air molecules are in the first ten miles above sea level. Nearly all the rest are in the next 40 miles. Scientists have discovered this by using balloons and rockets to lift weather instru-

3

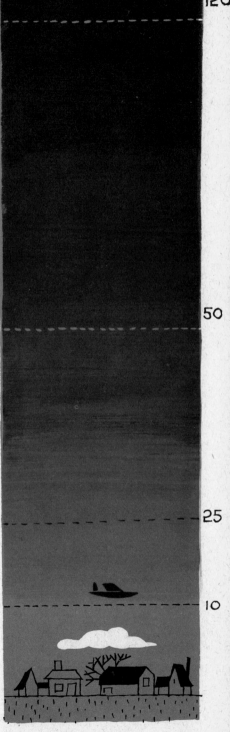

ments attached to little radio broadcasting sets. These instruments report automatically. One set was lifted 250 miles by a WAC Corporal rocket, and it broadcast signals which showed there is some very, very thin air even at that height.

Higher up, scarcely any air remains. Have you ever watched the northern lights on a cold, clear night? These shining streamers and curtains of light are made when electric particles from the sun shoot through very thin air, causing it to glow. The highest northern lights ever seen were about 700 miles above the earth, so there must be a little air up there. No one knows how much farther it goes. Where it ends, space begins. In space there is nothing that can light up, nothing that can become warm. Space has no weather. It is always dark and cold.

All the air that lies between the earth and space is called the **atmosphere.** It forms a flimsy but marvelous covering for our planet. Fortunately for us, the earth's gravity is strong enough to keep the atmosphere from drifting away. No molecule — or anything else — can fly into space unless it goes up faster than gravity pulls it down. And very few gas molecules ever shoot upward fast enough to overcome gravity.

Because gravity pulls air molecules downward, the upper atmosphere squeezes the lower part into a shallow layer. This is why air is thickest near the ground.

The push of the horde of air molecules against each other and against the earth is called **atmospheric pressure.** The weatherman has to measure atmospheric pressure, and to do it he uses a **barometer.** This instrument shows that the atmosphere pushes on a square inch of ground at sea level with about the force of a 15-pound weight. So we know that at sea level the air between a square inch of ground and space weighs about 15 pounds. (High up, the air is thinner, and pressure is less.)

As you walk around, you are like a juggler balancing a stick on his nose. Your stick is a tall slender column of air that goes all the way from your nose to space. Trillions and trillions of gas molecules make this column. The weight of each molecule is very slight, but if you are at sea level and if your nose has two square inches of surface, all the molecules above it weigh about 30 pounds. If your shoulders have 20 square inches of surface, they balance a piece of sky weighing about 300 pounds. Yet the air you support is only a small part of the atmosphere. The whole atmosphere weighs more than five thousand times a trillion *tons!*

Usually you don't feel the atmosphere pressing on you. The blood in your veins and arteries, and the air in your chest, have pressure, too. This inside pressure balances the outside pressure and makes the atmosphere seem weightless.

But the atmosphere's pressure is real. This is how you can prove it.

Take a large clean metal can with a screw cap. Pour about one-half cup of water into the can and boil it. The water molecules spread out when they are heated, and form steam. The steam fills the space inside the can and drives out the air that is there.

When little clouds form above the can, turn off the heat. Screw on the cap quickly.

Using pot-holders, carry the can to the sink and run cold water over it. The can collapses with a groan.

6

Do you know how the can was crushed? When you cooled it, the steam turned from gas to liquid. Its molecules bunched close together and formed little drops. The liquid water took up less room than the steam. Since most of the air molecules had been driven out of the can, what air was left was very thin. Its pressure was much lower than that of the air outside. So the atmospheric pressure shoved in the sides of the can. But it can't do that to you! The pressure within your body balances that of the atmosphere.

Examine the crushed can and notice that the top, bottom, and sides all were pushed in. This shows that the atmosphere pressed on the can from all directions. Since the molecules that form the lower part of the atmosphere are packed down by the weight of those above them, they push back in all directions. It's as though they are trying to squeeze out from under the heavy pile of air on top of them.

Push aside some air and more takes its place. You can't punch a hole in the atmosphere, because the gas molecules are always moving. They fill whatever space they can reach.

7

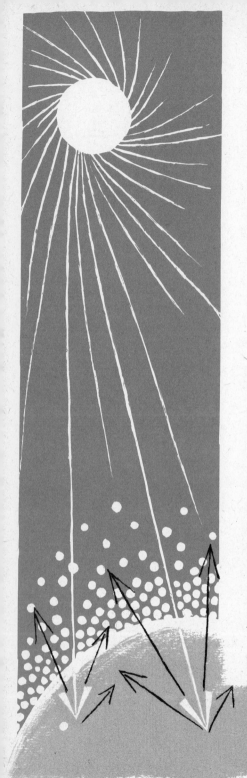

2. warming a planet

It is because the air is always moving that we have weather. If the air stayed still, we would have no wind, no rain or snow.

But what makes the air move? The answer is **heat.** The sun, which is about 93,000,000 miles away, supplies the heat. This ball of glowing gases is a hundred times wider than the earth, and its surface temperature is over 10,000 degrees!

The sun stays hot because it is a kind of atomic-energy powerhouse. It works all the time, producing enough energy to warm up many worlds. As the sun makes atomic energy, many kinds of invisible rays leave every part of its surface. These rays are not hot, and they shoot right through empty space. They produce heat or light only after they strike matter of some kind.

The rays travel from the sun at the great speed of 186,000 miles a second. Not all of them reach the earth. But those that do, arrive in less than 8½ minutes. Air molecules stop some of the rays that come here, but most of them pass through the atmosphere and hit the land and sea. The earth then becomes warmed up and sends off heat to the air. About nine tenths of the air's heat comes to it in this roundabout way.

8

The air warms up after the sun rises, and cools after the sun sets. During the night the temperature continues to fall, and in the morning it rises again.

The turning of the earth on its axis sets this rhythm. Whichever part of the earth faces the sun has day. Whichever part is turned away from the sun has night.

In the morning the earth turns us toward the sun, which then looks as if it were climbing up the sky. At noon we are almost directly under the sun and it appears high above us. In the afternoon, as we turn away from the sun, it seems to move down toward the horizon.

When the sun is low in the sky, its rays come toward us at a slant. The higher the sun, the less its rays slant. This makes an enormous difference in the amount of heat we receive.

Take a flashlight and shine it on dark or shady ground. First hold the light so that it throws a slanting beam. Then shine it directly on the ground. Notice that the direct beam covers less ground.

Sunbeams land in the same way. Each beam is made of separate rays. When a beam lands directly on a patch of ground, more rays hit the patch than when a slanting beam falls on it. So direct sunbeams deliver more heat.

While our planet spins on its axis, it also circles the sun. Each round trip takes one year. Since the earth's axis is tilted, first one half, then the other, leans toward the sun.

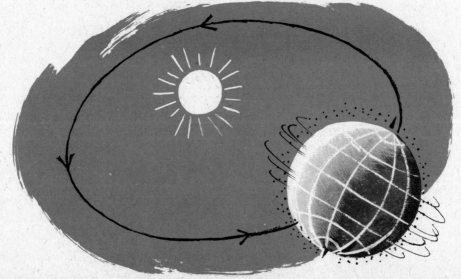

When our half of the earth is tilted toward the sun, we have summer. Days are longer than nights, and the sun is high in the sky for several hours a day. We receive more direct rays than at any other time of the year, and our part of the world becomes warm.

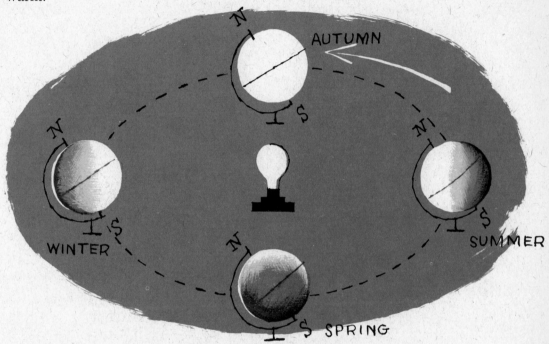

When the northern half of the earth leans away from the sun, our days are short. Even at noon the rays come toward us at a slant. So we receive less sunshine and the weather turns cold. It is winter. Meanwhile the people of the southern hemisphere have summer. All their seasons are the opposite of ours.

Carry a globe around a light, as shown in the picture, and you will see why the seasons change.

3. weather and climate

Whatever the seasons, we still have changing weather. Not all summer days are equally hot; not all winter days are equally cold. One day is wet; another day is dry. Since weather is always changing everywhere, we cannot compare it in different places. But we can record the daily temperatures of a place for a year and figure out the average yearly temperature. We can do the same with rainfall. This gives us the average yearly weather, which can be compared with that in other parts of the world. The average yearly weather of a place is called its **climate.**

The earth's hottest places are around the equator because this region has the most sunshine. Regions around the two poles have the least sunshine, so they are coldest. In between the hottest and coldest zones are two rather mild regions.

Look at the drawing on page 11 and you can see why the equatorial zone has more sunshine than the others. At noon the sun's rays come almost straight down on it, no matter which way the earth's axis is tilted. In other zones the earth's surface curves away from the sun. For at least part of the year the noon rays hit at a slant, and fewer fall on each square foot of ground.

As the sun's rays fall on the earth, the land and sea heat up at different rates. Land heats up faster than water, as shown by this experiment.

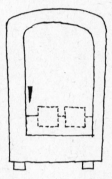

Take two coffee cans and fill one with dry soil and another with water. Set them in the refrigerator until both are about the same temperature.

Then place them outdoors in warm sunshine. Two hours later the soil will be warmer than the water. You can tell this just by touching them.

Land also cools off faster than water. If you visit a beach, you may find that the sand is quite cool in the early morning. By noon it may be too hot to walk on with bare feet. After sunset, the sand cools off again. If you test the water at different times during the day and night, you find its temperature doesn't change more than one or two degrees. Meanwhile the temperature of the land may change as much as 40 degrees.

The temperature of the sea is so steady that it doesn't change much from winter to summer. This is because a lot of heat is

needed to warm up water even a few degrees. Water stores heat. When winter comes, the sea still has some of the heat it stored during the summer. It is like someone who saves money and spends it cautiously.

But land is like a spendthrift. Easy come — easy go. Land uses up heat almost as fast as it is received, and stores very little. So land is warmer than the sea in summer and colder in winter.

Altitude — the height above sea level — also makes a difference in temperature. If you have ever climbed a high mountain, you know it is colder on top than down in the valley. Snow lingers on mountains long after it has disappeared from the lowlands. On the summits of very high mountains, snow lasts all through the year.

Two miles above sea level the temperature drops as much as 30 degrees. Up higher the air is still colder. For each thousand feet of altitude, up to about 40,000 feet, the normal drop in temperature is around three degrees. This is why. The bottom of the atmosphere is warmed from below by sun rays that hit the earth and are reflected as heat rays.

4. taking the air's temperature

Just how hot is the air around you? You can't tell from your own feelings. You need a measuring instrument — a **weather thermometer.**

The main part of a weather thermometer is a sealed glass tube that holds a liquid. The liquid may be mercury, which is silver in color, or it may be alcohol, dyed red. When warmed, the liquid expands and rises in the tube. When cooled, it shrinks and goes down. The tube is fixed against a background with a scale marked on it. The distance between each point on the scale is one degree.

The thermometer was invented about 350 years ago. At first it had no scale and was hard to use. Instrument makers set to work trying to improve it. One who succeeded was Daniel Gabriel Fahrenheit (FAR-en-hite) of Holland. In 1714 he invented the scale that now bears his name. On it the temperature of ice — that is, the point at which water freezes — is 32 degrees, and the boiling point of water is 212 degrees. This is the scale on your weather thermometer.

Fahrenheit's thermometer became known as the finest in the world, and scientists of many lands ordered instruments from him. Soon the **Fahrenheit scale** was in widespread use. Today it is the scale for weather work in the United States and the British Commonwealth of Nations.

Shortly after Fahrenheit invented his scale, two Swedish scientists worked out

the **centigrade scale.** Its zero mark is the freezing point of water. In many countries it is now the official scale. To avoid confusion, scientists write after a temperature reading the initial of the scale they have used.

When you see 32°F., you know the temperature was taken on a Fahrenheit thermometer. You read it, "Thirty-two degrees Fahrenheit." A temperature below zero is written with a minus sign in front of it — for example, -32° F. You read this, "Minus 32 degrees Fahrenheit."

Before using a thermometer for weather work, you must make sure it is accurate. To do this, you can use one of Fahrenheit's tests. Fill a glass with cracked ice and stick the bulb of the thermometer in it. The reading should be 32°F.

When you set your thermometer outside, keep it away from strong winds. Choose a north wall or some other place where sunlight never falls. If the sun shines on a thermometer, the rays heat it, so you can't tell the true temperature of the air.

5. what happens when air is heated

Air behaves like the liquid in a thermometer. Heat it and it expands; cool it and it shrinks. For proof, try this experiment.

Stretch part of a balloon over the mouth of a metal cup, and fix it in place with rubber bands. Set the cup on a toaster. Heat it for one minute. See the rubber puff out as the air in the cup expands. Use a pot-holder to remove the cup.

Set the cup in a refrigerator for a minute. When you remove it, notice that the rubber is pulled down into the cup. This shows the air inside has shrunk, or contracted.

All gases, liquids, and solids expand when heated and contract when cooled — some more and some less. This is explained by the behavior of molecules. **Heat energy** sets them in motion. The more heat there is, the faster they move, and the farther apart they spread. Cooling makes molecules slow down. As they lose their "pep" — their energy — they draw closer together.

A batch of cold, shrunken air will contain more molecules and be a little heavier than a warm batch of air of the same size. The thicker cold air will press harder against every square inch of surface that it touches. In other words, it will have more **pressure.**

In the study of weather, it is important to know whether the air pressure is rising or falling, for rain and snow storms usually develop only when air is losing some of its pressure. Your thermometer will give you some idea of the pressure changes taking place in the air. As the temperature goes down, the air pressure becomes greater. When the temperature rises, the air pressure becomes less.

6. barometers and how they work

A better way to keep track of air pressure is with a barometer. If you don't have one at home or at school, you can make a substitute.

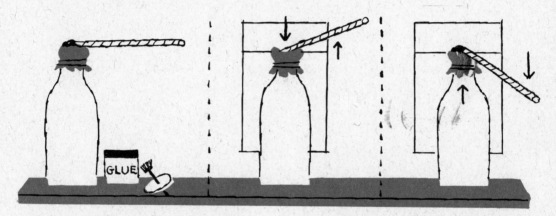

Cut a piece of balloon rubber big enough to fit tightly over the mouth of a quart milk bottle. Fix it there with a rubber band. Put a dab of glue on the balloon rubber about an inch from the edge of the bottle, and put one end of the straw on the glue, as shown in the picture.

With dabs of modeling clay mount a piece of cardboard, 8 by 10 inches in size, against the side of the milk bottle. Place the cardboard so that the position of the straw can be marked on it. Notice where the straw is when you first set up your barometer and mark this place on the card.

Keep your barometer indoors, away from a radiator. When the air outside the bottle becomes heavier than the air inside, the rubber will dent and the straw will rise. This is a sign fair weather may be due. If the air outside the bottle becomes lighter than the air inside, down goes the straw. If the temperature is above 32°, expect rain; but if it is below 32°, expect snow.

19

Aneroid barometer

Weathermen use a barometer that works somewhat like a homemade one. It has a can made of very thin metal. Air has been taken out of the can, so the barometer is called **aneroid,** or airless. Attached to the top of the can is a long pen. This writes on a clock-driven drum. The pen and drum correspond to the straw and cardboard in the homemade barometer. Weathermen study the lines made by the pen. From them they can tell if the air pressure is going up or down.

Many homes and ships use a simple aneroid barometer. This kind doesn't record changes, but just shows what the pressure is at the moment. It has a face and hand. As the hand moves around, it tells the pressure of the air.

More accurate than an aneroid is a **mercury barometer.** Weathermen use this kind, too. The main part of this instrument is a three-foot glass tube containing mercury. The tube is sealed on top, but open at the bottom and set in a small bowl of mercury. An increase in air pressure makes the mercury move up the tube; a decrease makes it move down. A scale set behind the tube shows the height of the mercury in inches. The air pressure is read in terms of inches of mercury.

Mercury barometer

Simple aneroid barometer

When the mercury in a barometer at sea level stands above 30 inches, the pressure is higher than normal. It may go as high as 32 inches or as low as 27.

Water can be used in a barometer, but since it is much lighter than mercury, air pressure drives it high up the tube. A few hundred years ago, a German mayor named Otto von Guericke made use of this fact, and built a water barometer that startled his neighbors.

Von Guericke ran a long pipe inside his house from the first floor through the roof. He put a tub at the bottom and filled the pipe with water. On top, the mayor floated a wooden dummy of a man, then covered the pipe with a glass dome.

When the air pressure was high, the dummy rose above the roof. But when the air pressure went down, the water level and the dummy disappeared down the pipe. Soon the villagers noticed that storms usually followed the dummy's disappearance and that fair weather was due when it popped out of the pipe.

Some people accused the mayor of witchcraft, but von Guericke calmed them by explaining why the dummy bobbed up and down.

21

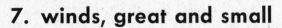

7. winds, great and small

Air pressure varies from place to place because temperature varies. But air is always moving, trying to even off the differences in pressure. Air pushes from an area of higher pressure to one of lower pressure, and this causes **wind.** The greater the difference in pressure between the two areas, the faster the wind.

The speed of the wind determines its force. You know that a fast-moving ball has more force than a slow-moving one. The same is true of the wind.

To tell the speed and force of a wind, notice what it does to the things in its path. If there is a flag of regular size nearby, watch it. In calm air the flag hangs against the staff. If the flag is one third of the way up, the wind is blowing at about 10 miles an hour. If the flag is two thirds of the way up, the wind is moving at 20 miles an hour. A wind that blows at 30 miles an hour makes a flag fly straight out from the mast.

Weathermen rate wind force and speed according to a twelve-point scale named after Admiral Beaufort, its inventor.

For a more accurate measurement of wind speed, weathermen have a special instrument, the **anemometer** (an-e-мoм-e-ter). It is a group of metal cups set on a shaft. When the wind blows into them, they turn while a meter clocks their speed.

Winds may be small streams of air flowing through the atmosphere, or they may be mighty rivers. They may flow slowly or

22

THE BEAUFORT (BO-fert) SCALE

Scale Number	Name of wind	Miles per hour	What the wind does
0	Calm	Less than 1	Smoke goes straight up
1	Light air	1-3	Smoke is slightly bent
2	Light breeze	4-7	Leaves rustle; wind vane moves
3	Gentle breeze	8-12	Leaves and twigs in constant motion
4	Moderate breeze	13-18	Raises dust and paper; moves small branches
5	Fresh breeze	19-24	Small trees begin to sway
6	Strong breeze	25-31	Large branches in motion
7	Moderate gale	32-38	Whole trees sway; walking is difficult
8	Fresh gale	39-46	Breaks twigs off trees
9	Strong gale	47-54	Damages chimneys and roofs
10	Whole gale	55-63	Trees uprooted. (Rare inland)
11	Storm	64-75	Widespread damage. (Very rare inland)
12	Hurricane	Above 75	Most destructive of all winds

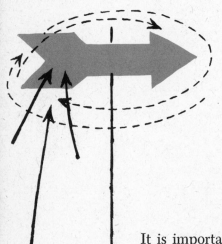

swiftly. And they may come from any direction.

Long ago, sailors named the winds according to the direction from which they blew. Since the sailors depended on the winds' power to drive their ships across the seas, they gave the winds second names which told their strength. We still do this today. When we speak of a **northeast gale,** we mean a furious wind from the northeast. A **south breeze** means a gentle wind from the south.

It is important to know the winds, for they bring the weather. In our part of the world, the air is seldom calm. Watch carefully and you notice some wind. One way to tell its direction is to stand in a big open space and turn your face until you feel the wind against one cheek. Another way is to watch smoke coming from chimneys. Best of all is to watch a weather vane.

The correct name for this instrument is **wind vane.** It is an arrow with a broad end, mounted on a high pole. More air strikes the broad end than the point. So the vane is pushed around until its point faces the direction from which the wind is coming.

Streams of air flow like streams of water. Whirlpools, or eddies, often develop in them. If a wind has a lot of little eddies in it, weathermen say it is **gusty.** They wait for the gusts to pass before observing wind direction. You will want to do this, too.

8. how a wind starts

A **local wind** is a small air stream blowing across a small area. It forms as heavy, high-pressure, cool air pushes light, low-pressure, warm air out of place. The best way to see how a local wind develops is to make one in your own kitchen. Here's how to do it.

First close the windows. Then light some of the burners on the stove and open the refrigerator. To trace the flow of air, use a smoke jar. For this, you need a quart jar with a cover. Take a piece of cardboard six inches long, and light one end. Quickly drop it into the jar and put on the lid. Uncover the jar near the bottom of the open refrigerator. Smoke from the jar will mark the direction of air flow. The smoke trails downward toward the floor, showing that cold, heavy air from the icebox is sinking. Let out some smoke over the stove, and you will see that the air there is rising.

The two currents work together. The cold air spreading along the floor has more pressure than the air there, so it shoves that air toward the stove. This sideways movement of the air is a wind.

The air over the stove expands as it is heated, and it becomes light enough to float on top of the heavy, cold air. But soon the heated air cools off and begins to shrink. So, after a while, it starts falling, causing a down current.

Outdoors, air flows from a colder to a warmer place in the same way, causing a local wind. Along with the low wind there is a rising air current — called an **updraft** — an **upper wind,** and a **downdraft.** This swirl of air is a **wind system.**

One of the most welcome local winds is the cool breeze that blows inland from the sea or a big lake on a hot summer day. Such a breeze develops because the land has a higher temperature than the water, and the air over it becomes warmer than that over the water. A low-pressure area forms over the land. Then the cooler air from above the water flows inland. This makes a breeze. At night, when the land is cooler, a breeze blows from land to sea.

9. planetary winds

A local wind, with its updraft, upper air stream, and downdraft, is like a little wheel turning inside a bigger one. When we are inside a local wind system, we don't notice the big general system. But weathermen do. They record wind direction day after day, and find that in the United States the winds blow mainly from a westerly direction. These winds are called **prevailing westerlies.**

Our westerlies are planetary winds. They have a rather complicated history. Hot air from the equator rises and expands. Part of it moves toward the South Pole, and part toward the North Pole. By the time air has gone one third of the way to the North Pole, it is quite cool. It sinks, forming a downdraft. The downdraft then divides into a northbound and a southbound stream. The earth's spin keeps these streams from traveling due north and south. Both are bent, so that winds in the southbound stream become **easterlies,** and winds in the northbound stream become our prevailing westerlies.

The westerlies sweep across the United States. On meeting colder, heavier air from the north, they are forced to rise. As the diagram shows, our westerlies make the ground stream of a colossal wind swirl. In the southern hemisphere there is a similar wind system.

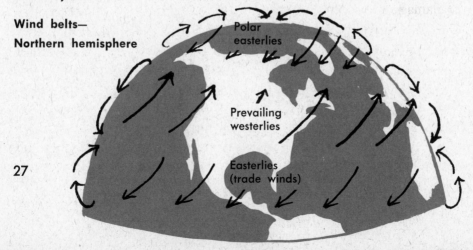

**Wind belts—
Northern hemisphere**

Polar
easterlies

Prevailing
westerlies

Easterlies
(trade winds)

27

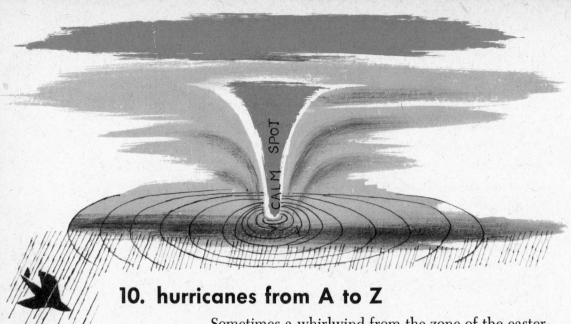

CALM SPOT

10. hurricanes from A to Z

Sometimes a whirlwind from the zone of the easterlies (also called the **trade wind belt**) invades our air and we have a **hurricane.** This type of storm is about 500 miles wide. Winds spiraling from the center carry thick clouds and heavy rains. The winds whirl at speeds of up to 150 miles an hour, while the whole storm advances at about 15 miles an hour. The average life of a hurricane is nine days. In that time it may travel a few thousand miles.

Hurricanes die as they head inland, but in their death throes they batter down trees and buildings. They cause towering sea waves which pound against the coast and do almost as much damage as the wind.

Weathermen keep track of hurricanes with radar, and also explore them by flying right into them. Toward the center the plane is tossed about violently. Suddenly it moves into smooth, calm air. The plane has entered an open area, with blue sky overhead, encircled by towering walls of cloud. This is the **eye,** the center of the hurricane, around which the winds rage.

Each hurricane is given a name — a girl's name — taken from an alphabetical list. The first hurricane of the season receives the first name, which begins with A; the second, the name beginning with B; and so on. Each year a new list of names is prepared. But the weathermen don't have to keep thinking up names beginning with Q, X, or Z. Usually no more than twelve hurricanes reach us in a year, so only the names to L are used, and the others can be saved for the next season.

11. tornado!

A **tornado,** like a hurricane, is a whirlwind, but it is much narrower and its course is much shorter. This type of storm may start when dry cold air moving from a westerly direction overruns unusually warm, moist air from the south. Thick black clouds form, and there are thunderstorms.

Suddenly a gust of warm air rises with a spiraling motion. Soon this updraft is whirling at a speed of two or three hundred miles an hour. Water vapor is swept upward and in cooling forms a twisting, funnel-shaped cloud. This cloud is the trademark of the tornado, the most violent and freakish of all winds.

Angry cold air lashes around the outside of the funnel, causing a roar that can be heard for miles. The funnel sweeps over the earth like a giant vacuum cleaner. The updraft creates very low pressure within the funnel. As it passes over houses and barns, they sometimes explode because the higher pressure inside of them blows out their walls. Trains may be sucked up from their tracks, and trucks may be lifted and whirled around. It is said

BETH

DORIS

EDNA

GERT

HELEN

29

that tornadoes have snatched babies from their cribs and dropped them safely in treetops.

There's only one good thing to be said about a tornado: it is small. Less than a mile wide, as a rule, it runs a course of about 4½ miles. Its average life is 8 minutes. It travels so fast that it passes any point along its path in about 15 seconds.

Because a tornado is a small storm, weathermen can't pinpoint a spot where one may break. But they generally can tell when a region will be threatened. They warn of the danger, and people have time to take shelter in cellars.

Tornadoes have appeared in every state, but the Midwest has most of them. Even there, the chance of a tornado striking any particular spot is very slight.

12. water everywhere

Some people say our planet should be called Sea instead of Earth, for ocean water covers more than two thirds of its surface. The air also contains sea water, but in the form of the invisible gas called water vapor.

The sea is always drying up, but it is always filling up, too. Every day millions of tons of water leave the sea and go into the air, and every day nearly the same amount of water falls out of the air as rain or snow. Eventually rivers carry it back to the sea.

No matter how far inland you live, there are water molecules from all the oceans of the world in the air around you. Winds brought them to your neighborhood. Your local air also contains water vapor that was given off by the leaves of plants, and some that was breathed out by people and animals, as well as some that came from nearby lakes and rivers. But very often wind-blown molecules from the sea make up most of the water vapor in your local air.

If you had super-microscope eyes, you could see how liquid water turns to gas. The molecules of the liquid are quite lively. They jostle and bump one another, so a few of them are speeded up and move much faster than the rest. As this

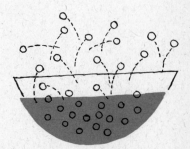

happens to molecules at the surface, some pop right into the air and form gas or vapor. In other words, they **evaporate.** If water is heated, its molecules gain energy and pick up speed. Then more of them evaporate.

Air may hold a great deal of water vapor and still be dry, for when water is a gas its molecules are far apart. They do not cling to things, and so they do not cause wetness. Air becomes damp only after some of its water molecules cool off, lose their energy, and collect in bundles to form drops of liquid.

When scattered water molecules gather together and form liquid, we say they **condense.** When the temperature is 32° F. or lower, water molecules line up and condense into ice. Water enters the air mixture by **evaporation,** but leaves it by **condensation.** Right now, both processes probably are going on in your neighborhood.

In a mass of air the size of a ten-story building covering a city block, there may be anywhere from 50 to 20,000 pounds of water in the form of gas. The amount of water vapor in the air is always changing, depending on the temperature. At any given temperature, air can hold just so much water vapor. When this limit is reached, air is **saturated** and will take no more. The higher the temperature of the air, the more water vapor it can hold. At 80°, air may contain 20 times as much moisture as at zero.

Perhaps you have noticed that on some days wet clothes dry faster than on others. The rate of drying, or evaporation, depends on how much water vapor is in the air compared to how much it could hold without changing in temperature.

32

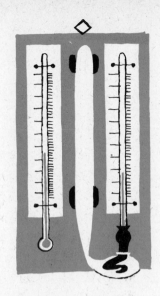

When clothes dry quickly, you know there is relatively little moisture in the air; but when they dry slowly, you know the air is almost saturated.

The amount of moisture in the air is called its **humidity.** It affects our comfort. Wet one finger and wave it in the air. Notice how cool it feels while it dries. This is because heat is used in turning water into vapor, and in this case the heat comes from your finger. When you sweat and the sweat dries, evaporation cools you off in the same way. If hot air hasn't too much moisture, your sweat evaporates rapidly and you feel comfortable. But if the humidity is high, evaporation is slow and you stay hot. Then you are likely to hear people complain, "It's not the heat but the humidity!"

The weatherman has a clever way of finding out how much more moisture the air can hold. He uses an instrument made of two thermometers. The bulb of one of these is covered by a piece of wet cloth, while the bulb of the other is uncovered. If the air is saturated, water won't evaporate from the cloth, and both thermometers will give the same reading. But if the air isn't saturated, water evaporates from the cloth. This cools the **wet-bulb thermometer** and it gives a lower reading than the **dry-bulb thermometer** does. If the air can hold a great deal more moisture, evaporation is rapid, and there is a big difference in the readings of the two thermometers. The amount of difference in the readings indicates **relative humidity,** or the amount of moisture actually in the air compared to the amount it could hold without changing temperature.

Saturated air is said to have a relative humidity of 100 per cent. If it has three fourths of the amount of moisture it can hold, its relative humidity is 75 per cent; if it has only one half the amount, its relative humidity is 50 per cent; and so on.

A weatherman notes difference in wet and dry bulb readings, then he consults a table from which he quickly learns the relative humidity. If this is very low, he expects a clear, cloudless sky. But if the relative humidity is high, a slight drop in temperature may cause clouds and then rain or snow.

Difference in dry and wet bulb readings	Temperature of air recorded by dry bulb											
	−10	0	10	20	30	40	50	60	70	80	90	100
1	55%	71%	80%	86%	90%	92%	93%	94%	95%	96%	96%	97%
2	10%	42%	60%	72%	79%	84%	87%	89%	90%	92%	92%	93%
3	—	13%	41%	58%	68%	76%	80%	84%	86%	87%	88%	90%
4	—	—	21%	44%	58%	68%	74%	78%	81%	83%	85%	86%
6	—	—	—	16%	38%	52%	61%	68%	72%	75%	78%	80%
8	—	—	—	—	18%	37%	49%	58%	64%	68%	71%	74%
10	—	—	—	—	—	22%	37%	48%	55%	61%	65%	68%
12	—	—	—	—	—	8%	26%	39%	48%	54%	59%	62%
14	—	—	—	—	—	—	16%	30%	40%	47%	53%	57%
16	—	—	—	—	—	—	5%	21%	33%	41%	47%	51%
18	—	—	—	—	—	—	—	13%	26%	35%	41%	47%
20	—	—	—	—	—	—	—	5%	19%	29%	36%	42%
22	—	—	—	—	—	—	—	—	12%	23%	32%	37%
24	—	—	—	—	—	—	—	—	6%	18%	26%	33%

humidity indicators

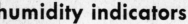

"Sweat" on a pitcher of ice water

Drops of water form on a pitcher of ice water as moisture from the air cools and condenses on the outside of the glass. Take a pitcher of ice water outdoors; wipe the glass dry. If drops form quickly, the air is nearly saturated and a fall-out of water can be expected. But if drops form slowly, the relative humidity is low and the weather will probably be fair.

Homemade wet and dry bulb thermometers

To make a wet bulb thermometer, cut off the tips of a white cotton shoe lace and boil it to remove impurities from the cloth. Then fit one end over the bulb of a thermometer. Set the other end in a small bottle of water. Mount this thermometer next to a dry bulb thermometer and take both outdoors. To speed up evaporation, blow on or whirl the bulb. To find the relative humidity, use the table on page 34.

The weather house

The man and woman who "live" in the house are tied together by a twisted cord of catgut. When the relative humidity is high, the cord soaks up water molecules from the air. Then it stretches and unwinds, and the woman comes out of the house while the man goes inside. He comes out when the humidity is low and the cord tightens up.

Weather flowers

Changes in humidity cause paper flowers that have been dipped in cobalt chloride solution to change color — pink when the humidity is high, and blue when it is low. Buy a small amount of cobalt chloride from a druggist, or get it from a chemistry set. Dissolve it in water to make a deeply colored solution. Dip a pink flower in the solution. After the flower dries, it will be a weather indicator if used outdoors.

13. dew and frost

Water in the air often condenses near the ground. Sometimes it makes **dew,** which forms on grass, flowers, and low bushes during clear summer nights. These things cool off quickly. The ground cools very quickly, too, chilling the lowest layer of the air until it is nearly saturated. Then water molecules in the chilled air collect on the colder ground surfaces and form dewdrops.

Dew does not form when there is wind because then the air close to the ground becomes mixed with warmer air. Clouds prevent dew from forming because they act like blankets and keep both ground and air from cooling off.

Dew forms only when the temperature is above 32°F. If it is 32° or lower, the water vapor freezes directly into ice crystals. Then **frost** forms. You sometimes see it on windowpanes, sidewalks, and on the ground, as well as on plants.

14. fog and smog

Sometimes a swarm of tiny water droplets gathers in the air near the ground, making a **fog**. The droplets form when cold ground cools the air above it so that its water vapor condenses. Fog particles are so small that thousands of them are needed to make a line one inch long. When the temperature is very cold, fogs can form from bits of ice.

At sea, fogs generally gather when warm, moist air blows over a cold current. Land fogs, "thick as pea soup," may form when winds blow warm sea air across colder land.

Smog is a city product, caused by dirty air. Its name is a combination of the words "smoke" and "fog." It forms when moisture collects around smoke particles. In recent years, the city of Los Angeles has been bothered by a special type of smog caused by a chemical from gasoline vapor.

Smogs are ugly, and unhealthy too. The way to prevent them is to avoid dirty air, that is, "pollution." Scientists have not yet found the best way of doing this, but they are at work on the problem.

37

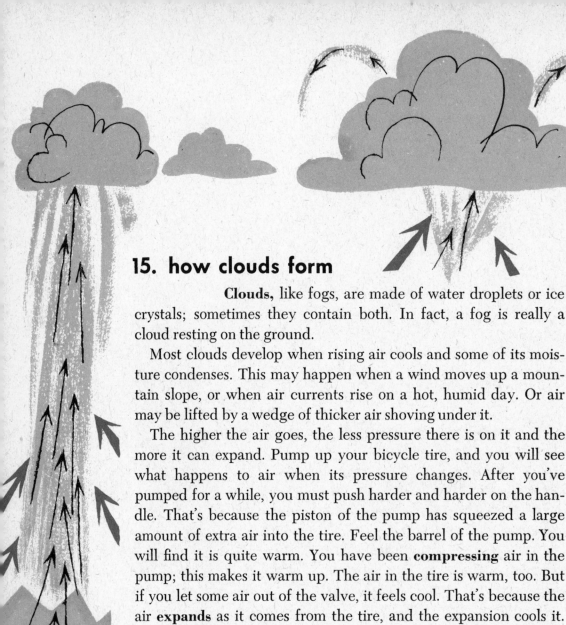

15. how clouds form

Clouds, like fogs, are made of water droplets or ice crystals; sometimes they contain both. In fact, a fog is really a cloud resting on the ground.

Most clouds develop when rising air cools and some of its moisture condenses. This may happen when a wind moves up a mountain slope, or when air currents rise on a hot, humid day. Or air may be lifted by a wedge of thicker air shoving under it.

The higher the air goes, the less pressure there is on it and the more it can expand. Pump up your bicycle tire, and you will see what happens to air when its pressure changes. After you've pumped for a while, you must push harder and harder on the handle. That's because the piston of the pump has squeezed a large amount of extra air into the tire. Feel the barrel of the pump. You will find it is quite warm. You have been **compressing** air in the pump; this makes it warm up. The air in the tire is warm, too. But if you let some air out of the valve, it feels cool. That's because the air **expands** as it comes from the tire, and the expansion cools it.

Outdoor air works the same way. When it descends, it compresses and warms up. When it rises, it expands and cools off. But cool air cannot hold as much water vapor as warm air. If the tempera-

38

ture falls so low that the air can no longer carry its load of water vapor, some of the vapor condenses into droplets, or, if the air is cold enough, into ice crystals. At that moment a cloud is born.

You can make a little cloud in a milk bottle and watch it form. Here's how to do it.

Using warm water, wet the inside of a clean milk bottle. Drop a lighted match into the bottle. It goes out immediately, but leaves a trail of smoke. The smoke supplies specks around which the moisture can condense.

Stand with your back toward the light so you can see what happens. Suck air out of the bottle and a cloud forms inside.

When you sucked air from the bottle, the remaining air expanded to fill up the space, and it became a little cooler. This made the water vapor condense and form a cloud of droplets. When you let fresh air into the milk bottle, the cloudy air was compressed and warmed. So the droplets evaporated.

Now you can see why falling air pressure usually means a storm is on the way. The air is expanding and cooling. This makes water vapor condense into water droplets which form clouds. But when pressure is rising, air is compressing and warming up. Cloud droplets then turn to vapor and the sky clears.

types of clouds

Weathermen divide the cloud-bearing part of the sky into three levels, and speak of "low," "middle," and "high" clouds. The levels are like the floors of a skyscraper. The "first floor" goes up to 6,500 feet. The "second floor" extends from 6,500 feet to 20,000 feet. The "third floor" runs from 20,000 to 40,000 feet.

Although no two clouds look exactly alike, they can be grouped into types.

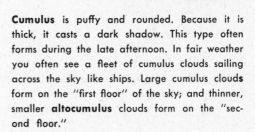

Stratus forms in an even sheet when the air is calm. Its underside is gray because it is in the shade. But the upper side, when seen from an airplane, looks like a sea of white foam. Stratus forms on the "first floor" of the sky. A thinner type called **altostratus** forms on the "second floor."

Cumulus is puffy and rounded. Because it is thick, it casts a dark shadow. This type often forms during the late afternoon. In fair weather you often see a fleet of cumulus clouds sailing across the sky like ships. Large cumulus clouds form on the "first floor" of the sky; and thinner, smaller **altocumulus** clouds form on the "second floor."

A combination cloud called **cirrostratus** forms on the "third floor." It appears as an even sheet that gives the sky a milky color, but it is so thin that it hardly dims the sun and moon. Another combination cloud, **cirrocumulus**, forms in small white balls or flakes, which look something like fish scales. Fishermen call them a "mackerel sky."

Cirrus clouds are the white wisps you often see high in the sky on clear days. They are made of ice particles and are too thin to cast a shadow. The sun and moon shine right through them. No rain or snow falls from them, for they contain little water. They form on the "third floor" of the sky.

Cumulus or stratus clouds may become carriers of rain or snow. Then **nimbus**, meaning "rain cloud," is added to their names. Stormy stratus is called **nimbostratus;** stormy cumulus is called **cumulonimbus.**

16. raindrops

       If air is saturated, clouds form quickly. Droplets condense in about 1½ minutes. We know **raindrops** take much longer to develop, although exactly how they form is still a mystery.

       Each raindrop contains about a million times as much water as a cloud droplet. You might think that little droplets come together and make big ones. But the droplets do nothing of the sort. They drive each other away. So do ice particles in a cloud.

       From laboratory experiments, weathermen know that in the atmosphere water sometimes remains liquid after its temperature falls below 32°. As they put it, water may become **supercooled.** When mixed with ice crystals, supercooled droplets evaporate quickly and the vapor freezes onto the crystals.

       Weathermen believe the same thing may happen in clouds. Each tall rain cloud has a top section made of ice crystals and a bottom section made of water droplets. In the middle, there is a supercooled section made of both. There, perhaps, the droplets turn to vapor. Then molecules of vapor freeze around ice crystals, making snowflakes. When these become too big and heavy to be supported by rising air currents, they fall. If the lower air is warm, the flakes melt on the way down and turn to raindrops.

Very large drops split while falling. The largest raindrops—the kind that patter as they land—are rarely more than 1/10 of an inch wide. The smallest are about 1/50 of an inch wide. Drops below that size are called **drizzle.**

Accurate measurements of raindrops are difficult to make. But here's how you can get some idea of their size.

First take an eyedropper and measure its width with a ruler. This will give you the size of the drops that fall from it. Hold the eyedropper high above a pan of flour and squeeze a row of drops from it.

Use aluminum foil to cover the doughballs that form, then set the pan outdoors for a moment and let raindrops splash on the flour. To tell how big they are, compare the doughballs they make with the set from measured drops.

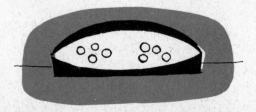

17. thundershowers

Sometimes hot, humid air rises in swirling currents. As it climbs, water condenses, making a billowy cumulus cloud. Higher up, where moisture freezes, strands of cirrus form. They crown the head of the cumulus. As more moisture comes to the cloud, its base spreads and darkens. Now it is a cumulonimbus cloud that can produce lightning.

Powerful air currents sweep through it. As raindrops and snowflakes are tossed about, they become charged with electricity. There are two kinds of charges, **positive** (shown by a plus sign) and **negative** (shown by a minus sign). They develop in different parts of the cloud but have a strong attraction for each other.

Suddenly the negative charges puncture a pathway toward the positive ones and rush madly toward them. This movement is an electric current. The current excites nearby air molecules, making them glow for a fraction of a second. We see their fleeting glow as **lightning.**

43

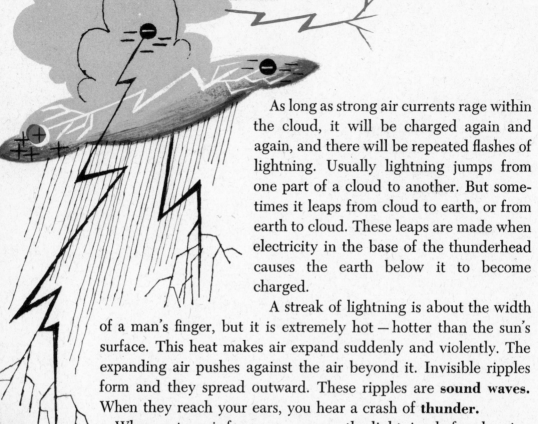

As long as strong air currents rage within the cloud, it will be charged again and again, and there will be repeated flashes of lightning. Usually lightning jumps from one part of a cloud to another. But sometimes it leaps from cloud to earth, or from earth to cloud. These leaps are made when electricity in the base of the thunderhead causes the earth below it to become charged.

A streak of lightning is about the width of a man's finger, but it is extremely hot — hotter than the sun's surface. This heat makes air expand suddenly and violently. The expanding air pushes against the air beyond it. Invisible ripples form and they spread outward. These ripples are **sound waves.** When they reach your ears, you hear a crash of **thunder.**

When a storm is far away, you see the lightning before hearing the thunder. That's because light travels faster than sound. To tell how many miles away a storm is, count the seconds between a lightning flash and its thunderclap, then divide by five. It takes about a second to pronounce four syllables, so you can count by saying "One million one, one million two, one million three," and so on.

Thunderstorms usually move about one-half mile a minute. One that is two miles away, and moving toward you, will arrive in four minutes. In that time you can seek shelter.

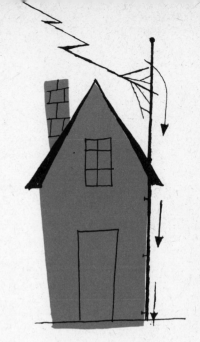

The safest place to be is in a car, a metal building, or one with a steel framework. If lightning strikes, the metal quickly carries the electricity to the ground. Lightning rods work in the same way. If properly set up, they give almost complete protection to wooden buildings.

If you must stay outdoors during a thunderstorm, seek a low place. Keep out of water, for if it is struck, electricity shoots through it. Another good rule is: avoid trees. When a tree is struck, the heat turns its sap to steam, which may split the wood and knock down parts of the tree.

Guard against lightning, then don't worry about it. Enjoy it. No man-made fireworks are as thrilling.

After a thunderstorm there may be a **rainbow.** Its beautiful colors are made by sunbeams passing through raindrops.

As long as the rainbow colors of the sun's rays are mixed, they make white light. But on passing through raindrops, the rays are bent. Red is bent the least, orange a little more, and so on. As a result, the rays' colors are separated, and the red, orange, yellow, blue, green, and violet of a rainbow result.

If you are to see a rainbow, your back must be toward the sun and your eyes toward the rain clouds. No one else can see through the same group of drops that you look through, so no two people ever see exactly the same rainbow.

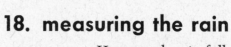

18. measuring the rain

How much rain falls during a storm? To determine this, a weatherman finds out the thickness of the water layer that would form if the rain piled up on level ground. He does this with an instrument called a **rain gauge.** The best way to understand how a rain gauge works is to make and use one. Here's how to do it.

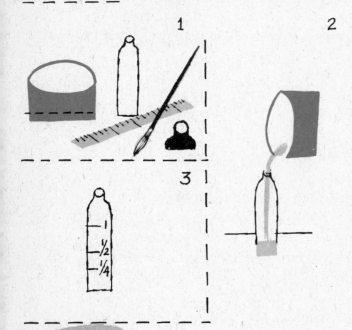

You will need these materials: black paint, a fine brush, a tall narrow olive bottle, a ruler, and a can about 8 inches wide.

Mark the gauge this way: Pour water into the can until it is one inch deep. Then pour this water into the olive bottle. Mark its level on the outside with black, and write 1″. Empty the bottle, then pour ½ inch of water from the can to the bottle. Mark its level. Repeat, but this time pour ¼ inch of water into the bottle and mark its level.

This is how you use the gauge: Set the can in an open place and fix it so it won't tip over. At the end of a storm, measure the rainfall by pouring the water from the can into the olive bottle.

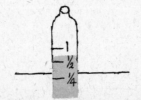

Unless you live in a dry state, you will find that one inch of rainfall is not unusual. Sometimes the rainfall will be less; sometimes more.

19. the rain-makers

To produce rain for several hours, clouds must have new supplies of moisture. Updrafts feed them, and so new rain-drops form and fall. When the updrafts stop, the storm dies down.

Raising tons of water to a rain cloud requires a tremendous amount of energy. This is provided by the sun, which has heated the air and given it lifting power.

Scientists think it would be foolish to try to copy nature's method of rain-making. "There may be an easier way," they say. "Perhaps we can work on the clouds and make them give up their moisture."

In recent years, some scientists have been testing a method called **cloud-seeding.** This is how it works in the laboratory. A little cloud is made, then supercooled with dry ice. This stuff is often used in packing ice cream, because it is colder than ordinary ice. When dry ice is added to the cloud, some ice crystals form. Water in droplets evaporates and freezes around the ice crystals. They grow, then fall as snowflakes.

Scientists have also discovered that a cool little cloud can be seeded with a chemical that is called silver iodide. Crystals of this

30.000 FT.

20.000 FT.

chemical are so much like ice crystals they attract water vapor, which freezes around them. Then snowflakes form and fall.

But does cloud-seeding work outdoors? Since 1946, scientists have been flying over tall clouds and dusting them with dry ice or silver iodide. Sometimes showers start, though not always. Perhaps the snow and rain that follow cloud-seeding would have fallen anyhow. The method must be tested in many places and over long periods of time before we shall know if it works.

Meanwhile many of the people who live in dry regions often hire men to sprinkle dry ice or silver iodide on promising clouds, hoping to get rain from them. A strange question has come up. Who owns the clouds? Suppose Arizona ranchers get rain from a cloud that would, if left alone, have blown to New Mexico and delivered rain there. Would the ranchers be cloud robbers? We shall certainly need rules about sharing the rain if and when we have weather made to order.

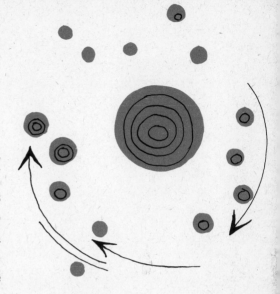

20. ice from the sky

On May 26, 1953, Washington, D. C., was pelted with **hailstones,** some as big as tennis balls. In them was radioactive material which was traced to an atomic explosion 29 hours earlier in Nevada. How it got into the hailstones is not known, for weathermen are not sure how hailstones are made.

Some scientists think that the rising air currents that feed a thunderhead carry raindrops up to the supercooled part of the cloud. There they turn into icy beads. Water molecules may freeze around the beads. Then, as they fall, some of this ice may melt. If the beads are tossed back up, more ice forms around them. As the hailstones are hurled up and down inside the thunderhead they may acquire many shells of ice.

Since hail forms only during thunderstorms, it is more common in summer than in winter. **Sleet,** however, is a cold-weather product. It forms when the air near the ground is 32° or lower, while the air above is warm enough to permit rain to pass through it. When the raindrops strike the colder lower air, they freeze into beads of sleet.

Ice storms occur when supercooled rain falls and freezes after it lands. Everything touched by the cold rain becomes glazed with ice. Because of its weight the ice may do great damage to trees and power lines.

21. snow

Snowflakes fall slowly and silently, for large amounts of air are trapped among their lacy crystals. Weathermen figure that a blanket of snow is usually nine parts air to one part water. To see how little water snow contains, fill a kitchen measuring cup with it, then let the snow melt. You will get about one tenth of a cup of water.

If you can, collect some snowflakes on a piece of black paper or cloth, then examine them with a magnifying glass. Each one looks like a piece of lace. No two are alike. Yet all are six-pointed or six-sided.

A snowflake begins as a single tiny crystal. Water vapor freezes around it, enlarging the crystal so that it becomes a small flat flake. This may fall, or it may grow by building new crystals as more water vapor freezes around it. But the flake can become large only if the temperature is just a few degrees below freezing. Very cold air has too little moisture to produce big flakes.

22. weather on parade

Even though the weatherman knows the temperature, wind direction, humidity, and air pressure of the place where he is, how can he forecast tomorrow's weather?

This is where our great planetary winds, the prevailing westerlies, enter the weather picture. Mountain ranges and local wind systems may block the course of the prevailing westerlies and force these winds to flow over or around them. Yet the westerlies keep moving across the United States toward the Atlantic Ocean at an average speed of 500 miles a day in summer and 700 miles a day in winter. They bring most of our weather. Cold clear air that blows into Chicago one day may arrive in New York the next day. A storm that hits Oklahoma City in the morning usually reaches St. Louis by night.

Fair and clear for a few days, then cloudy for a few days — this is the usual weather pattern for most of the United States. It is caused by changes in atmospheric pressure. The westerlies carry along batches of air of different pressure. Weathermen call the high-pressure batches **highs** and the low ones **lows**. The highs and lows follow one another in an endless parade, each bringing its own kind of weather.

A high is like a mountain of air, with its summit in the central part. There the pressure is greatest; around the edges it is least. A low is like a valley between two mountains. It may be a long, narrow valley, or it may be wide.

As you would expect, air tends to flow from a high into a low. The earth's spin bends the course of the flow, however, so that winds whirl out from the center of the high. Meanwhile, downdrafts bring in fresh air from aloft. As this air falls, it is compressed and warmed. Then it can hold more water vapor, and whatever clouds are in it evaporate. You can tell when a high is moving into your neighborhood. The barometric pressure rises, the wind shifts, and the sky clears.

In a low, air whirls inward toward the center, where the pressure is least. It expands and cools on the way, so its moisture condenses and clouds form. When a low arrives, air pressure falls, the wind shifts, clouds appear, and a storm may follow.

Highs and lows are not permanent. As they march along, winds blow from the highs into the lows. The air mountains level off and the valleys fill up. The highs and lows disappear, but new ones form and replace the old.

There is a special kind of high that covers tens of thousands of square miles. Such a high develops over a vast, evenly heated expanse of sea or flat land. It is called an **air mass.** No air masses form over the United States, but they do develop over the Pacific Ocean, northern Canada, and the Gulf of Mexico. Air moving into

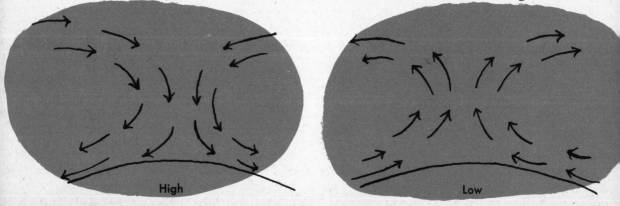

High   Low

one of these regions becomes sluggish. It may linger for nearly a week — long enough for its temperature and humidity to be affected by the area.

Over snowy northern plains, air turns cold and loses its moisture. It becomes a cold dry air mass. Over tropical seas, air becomes warm and laden with moisture. It forms a warm wet air mass. When an air mass starts moving, its temperature and humidity· traits are carried with it.

Every day at least one air mass reaches the United States. Each mass has traveled at its own speed and along its own path. But when it arrives here, the prevailing winds push it eastward.

Now and then the upper part of an air mass splits away from the lower part and goes its own way high above the ground. After a while it comes down to earth. In descending, it is compressed and heated. By the time the air reaches the ground, its clouds have evaporated and it has become hot. As this clear hot air settles over an area, it causes a **heat wave.**

When a very cold dry air mass arrives here from the Arctic, the temperature drops suddenly, and several states have a **cold wave.** This type of air mass travels fast, so a cold wave usually does not last long.

Hot and cold spells sometimes follow one another. Old-timers in Chicago can tell you of the time in 1911 when a man was overcome by the heat one day, and two men froze to death on the next day. Overnight the temperature dropped 61 degrees!

Air mass source regions

PACIFIC OCEAN

HAWAII

AZORES

ATLANTIC OCEAN

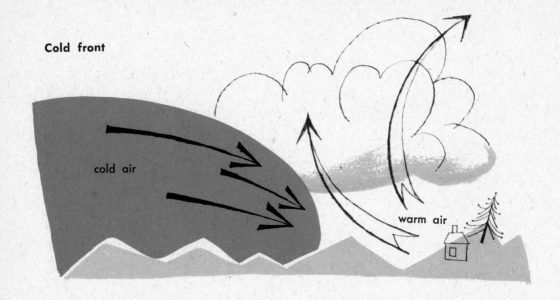

Cold front

cold air

warm air

23. battles between the air masses

Most of our storms develop when different kinds of air masses collide. The two air masses fight over the right of way. Usually the warmer air mass is forced to rise. It expands and cools rapidly, so that thick clouds form from its moisture. The clouds sweep across the sky and pour millions of gallons of water along their path.

Weatherman call the surface between clashing air masses a **front.** This is the battle line along which the air masses meet. You see a small-scale front when you open the door between a cold, unheated room and a warm room filled with smoky air. The heavy cold air wedges forward across the threshold, and pushes its way under the thin warm air. A sloping surface — a front — forms. The thin warm air slides over the front into the cold room, while the cold air creeps into the warm room.

An enormous sloping front forms when a cold dry air mass from Canada runs into a warm moist mass from the Gulf of Mexico. While the warm air is passing over your neighborhood, the temperature is high. The weather is fair, until suddenly a thunderhead appears. This is the sign that the front has arrived. While it is moving overhead the warm air rises, expands, and cools, and there is heavy rain or snow. Then the air mass from the north spreads over your neighborhood, bringing with it clear cold weather.

This type of front is called a **cold front** because it forms when a cold air mass overtakes a warm one. It is followed by colder weather. But sometimes a warm air mass overtakes a colder one, and a **warm front** develops, followed by warmer weather.

Spotting a front is difficult, even for weathermen. One way to tell that a front is passing overhead is to watch the barometer. The pressure goes down as the rising air expands. Another clue is the sudden appearance of storm clouds. After the front has passed and a new air mass arrives, the barometer rises and becomes steady, then the sky clears.

warm air

cold air

Warm front

24. forecasters at work

A **daily weather map,** somewhat like the one you see in the newspaper or on TV, is one of the main tools used by our forecasters. The map is a portrait of the atmosphere, caught in one particular fleeting moment. It shows the features of the air near the ground — the winds, the highs and lows, and the fronts.

Preparing the weather map is a big job. It takes teamwork. The U. S. Weather Bureau, which has more than six hundred stations scattered throughout the country, organizes the work.

Each day, at the same moment, government weathermen are at their stations making observations. They note the clouds, take wind direction and speed, and measure the temperature, air pressure, and humidity. If rain or snow has fallen, they measure that too. All this information is teletyped to a collecting office and recorded on a master map.

Weathermen are probably the greatest code-users in the world. But there is nothing secret about their code. It is international and can be read by anyone, regardless of his language. Weather-

men developed it so that the bureaus of different countries could exchange information.

Code numbers are used in sending reports into the collecting office. The numbers are arranged in groups of five. The meaning of each one depends on its position in the group, and on which group it is in. For example, a message may read: 40530 83220 12716 24731 67228 74542.

The 405 stands for the number of the reporting station, which, in this case, is Washington, D. C. The 30 following is the temperature at which condensation takes place. In the next group, 8 means "very cloudy"; 32 refers to wind direction and means "320 degrees," which is northwest; 20 stands for "20 knots an hour," the speed of the wind. Each of the other numbers also has a definite meaning.

At the collecting office the numbers are decoded and put on the map in picture language. Reporting stations are shown as small circles, and the symbols that describe their weather are arranged around them. Lines are drawn between stations with the same pressure. The pressure reading is marked beside each line. These lines, as a rule, form loops, resting one inside another. If a nest of

loops encloses a low, the center is labeled L. If it encloses a high, the center is labeled H.

After the station reports have been recorded, the men who prepare the daily weather map locate the fronts. They find them wherever there is a string of stations with high temperatures near a string of stations with lower temperatures. A different symbol is used for marking each type of front.

After the map is completed, a wirephoto of it is sent to the forecasting centers. Then it is rushed to the Government Printing Office, where thousands of copies are run off. These are mailed to subscribers.

When a forecaster looks at the day's weather map, he tries to figure out where the highs and lows and fronts will be tomorrow. He looks at the weather maps of the past few days and compares them with the latest map. He knows that the air masses and their fronts are likely to continue traveling at the same speed and in the same direction for another twenty-four hours. Since their average speed is 25 miles an hour, he has some idea where they will be by the next day.

The forecaster also studies the local air pressure and wind direction and speed. Perhaps something is happening in the air around his station that will change the course of an approaching pressure center. He checks the barometer, the thermometer, and all other "ometers" for the latest readings.

When he has a picture in his mind of the next day's weather map and how it will look, he writes out the forecast. Off it goes to the newspapers, radio stations, and TV studios. And soon everyone knows what kind of weather to expect, and plans accordingly.

To understand how the loops outline highs and lows, take a glass dessert dish and paint rings around the outside. Set the dish upside down on a map of the United States, and you will see how a high should really look. Imagine that the painted rings slip down onto the map. The rings now become the loops around a high.

Turn the dish right side up, and you will see how a low should really look. Again imagine that the rings slip down onto the map, giving the pattern of a loop.

Notice that the wind signs on the map are lined up in a way that shows how air spirals around high- and low-pressure areas. If you have a good imagination, you can almost feel the wind blowing outward from a high and inward toward a low.

The heavy black lines with jutting teeth mark the fronts. The juts are placed on the side toward which the front is moving. Their meaning is given below.

warm front
cold front
stationary front — a boundary between two air masses that are almost standing still
occluded front — a front along which a wedge of warm air has been lifted by two opposing air masses.

Sky coverage	
○	No clouds
◑	Less than one-tenth or one-tenth
◔	Two and three-tenths
◔	Four-tenths
◑	Five-tenths
◕	Six-tenths
◕	Seven and eight-tenths
◕	Nine-tenths or overcast with openings
●	Completely overcast
⊗	Sky obscured

Force of wind

	Miles per hour			Miles per hour
◎	Calm			44 - 49
	1 - 4			50 - 54
	5 - 8			55 - 60
	9 - 14			61 - 66
	15 - 20			67 - 71
	21 - 25			72 - 77
	26 - 31			78 - 83
	32 - 37			84 - 89
	38 - 43			119 - 123

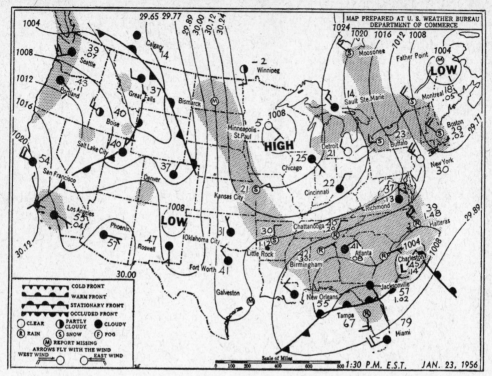

Courtesy of The New York Times

reading a weather map

The weather map you see in your daily paper is a simple one drawn from the more complicated U. S. Weather Bureau map. On it you will find symbols that look like music notes. Each circle represents one of the reporting weather stations, and its staff points *into* the wind. Lines on the staff give the force of the wind (See page 60). In many newspapers their meaning is given at the bottom of the map.

You will notice that some of the circles are all black, some are partly black, and some are white. The shading indicates how much cloudiness there is at the station, as explained by the table on page 60. Thus we know that at a station with a marking like this: ⊶ the sky is fair and there is a breeze of 5-8 miles an hour from the west.

The number beside each station indicates the temperature at the time of reporting. Figures in decimals under the temperature number show the amount of rain or snow (in inches) within the six hours prior to the time shown on the map. The gray shading on the map shows those areas which have had rain or snow within six hours.

The thin swirling lines connect points with the same air pressure, and numbers at the edge of the map show this pressure in millibars, which are units used by weathermen in measuring pressure.

At first it is hard to grasp the meaning of these loops on the weather map because it is flat, while the air has depth. Each high center is really the summit of an air mountain, while each low center is the bottom of a valley.

(over)

25. making your own forecasts

It's fun to try forecasting as the weathermen do it. Save the daily weather maps from your newspaper and compare them. Or if you wish to obtain the official daily weather map, write to the Superintendent of Documents, Washington, D. C., and say you want to subscribe for it. Enclose sixty cents in coin for a month's subscription, or $7.20 for a year's subscription.

Tack the maps of the past few days on a bulletin board or keep them in a notebook. Use them along with your barometer, and you will be able to follow the march of the highs and lows and the passing of fronts.

The table on the next page, prepared by a former chief of the U. S. Weather Bureau, is a good guide to forecasting for most of the United States. It can be used with a milk-bottle barometer, if you do not have a scale barometer. The movements of the straw will show whether the pressure is rising or falling. That's the important thing. Remember that falling pressure causes clouds and storms; and rising pressure brings fair, clear weather.

61

Wind direction	Pressure at sea level	Forecast
SW to NW	30.10-30.20 and steady	Fair for 1 or 2 days
SW to NW	30.10-30.20 and rising rapidly	Fair, followed by rain in 2 days
SW to NW	30.20 and above, and falling slowly	Slowly rising temperature, and fair for 2 days
SW to NW	30.20 and above, and stationary	Continued fair, with no decided temperature change
S to SE	30.10 to 30.20, and falling slowly	Rain within 24 hours
S to SE	30.10 to 30.20, and falling rapidly	Faster wind with rain in 12 to 24 hours
SE to NE	30.10 to 30.20, and falling slowly	Rain in 12 to 18 hours
SE to NE	30.10 to 30.20, and falling rapidly	Faster wind and rain in 12 hours
E to NE	30.10 and above, and falling slowly	In summer, rain may not fall for several days; in winter, rain in 24 hours
E to NE	30.10 and above, and falling rapidly	In summer, rain probably in 12 to 24 hours; in winter, rain or snow when barometer begins to fall
SE to NE	30.00 or below, and falling slowly	Rain for 1-2 days
SE to NE	30.00 or below, and falling rapidly	Rain and high wind; clearing in 36 hours
S to SW	30.00 or below, and rising slowly	Clearing in a few hours; and fair for several days
S to E	29.80 or below, and falling rapidly	Severe storm coming; clearing in 24 hours
E to N	29.80 or below, and falling rapidly	Severe NE gale and heavy rain; in winter, heavy snow
Going to W	29.80 or below, and rising rapidly	Clearing and colder

After making your prediction, write it down. Afterwards check it with the weatherman's forecast and with the weather itself. Both you and the weatherman may be wrong, but the weather will be right. It cannot be otherwise, for weather behaves according to the laws of nature.

index